WINGS

WINGS

THE EARLY YEARS OF AVIATION

by Richard Rosenblum

FOUR WINDS PRESS NEW YORK

LIBRARY OF CONGRESS CATALOGING IN PUBLICATION DATA

Rosenblum, Richard.
    Wings, the early years of aviation.

    Includes index.
    Summary: An illustrated history of airplanes from the days of the early
aviators through the beginning of World War II. Discusses the pilots,
their uniforms, famous planes, blimps, insignias, air races and circuses,
passenger service, and many other related topics.
    1. Aeronautics—Juvenile literature.
[1. Aeronautics] I. Title.
TL547.R63   629.13'009   79-26363
ISBN 0-590-07576-4

PUBLISHED BY FOUR WINDS PRESS
A DIVISION OF SCHOLASTIC MAGAZINES, INC., NEW YORK, N.Y
COPYRIGHT © 1980 BY RICHARD ROSENBLUM
ALL RIGHTS RESERVED
PRINTED IN THE UNITED STATES OF AMERICA
LIBRARY OF CONGRESS CATALOG CARD NUMBER: 79-26363
1 2 3 4 5 84 83 82 81 80

To my daughter, Anne

THE BEGINNING

People have always yearned to fly. From Daedalus and Icarus to Peter Pan, the urge to soar through the air is as old as humanity.

The great Renaissance artist Leonardo da Vinci designed the first "flying apparatus" as well as the first parachute and the first helicopter. By studying the mechanics of birds' wings, he began the science of flight. Later, people started experimenting with balloons. In 1873, a balloon filled with hot air and drifting with the wind was built and successfully carried passengers. Two years later, the English Channel had been crossed by balloon.

Throughout the nineteenth century, adventurers and scientists experimented with gliders of curious design. Still, controlled flight was the great goal. What was needed was a machine to give both power and direction. Some people tried harnessing eagles; others used treadmills or giant steam engines. In December of 1903, Samuel Pierpont Langley, the director of the Smithsonian Institution in Washington, D.C., came very close to controlled flight in an aircraft powered by a gasoline motor.

LEONARDO DA VINCI

DE LANA'S AIRSHIP ~ 1670

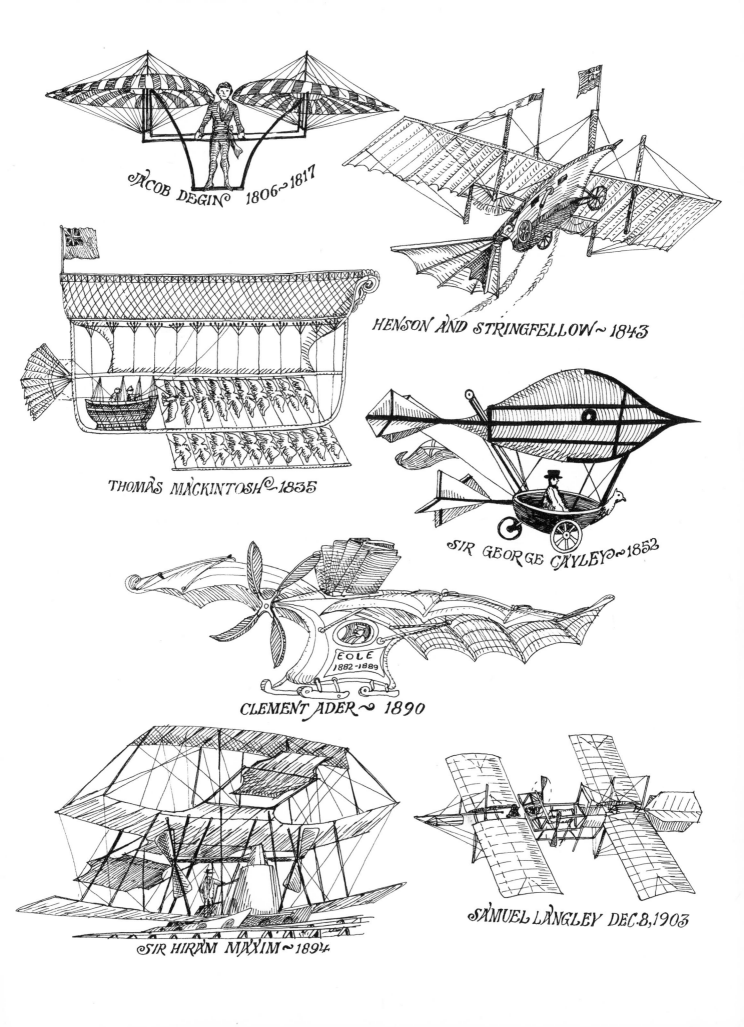

JACOB DEGIN   1806~1817

HENSON AND STRINGFELLOW ~ 1843

THOMAS MACKINTOSH ~ 1835

SIR GEORGE CAYLEY ~ 1852

EOLE
1882-1889

CLEMENT ADER ~ 1890

SIR HIRAM MAXIM ~ 1894

SAMUEL LANGLEY DEC. 8, 1903

Less than a month after Langley's attempt, two brothers, Wilbur and Orville Wright, decided that in spite of excessive winds, this would be the day. The brothers owned a bicycle shop in Dayton, Ohio, where they spent most of their time building and experimenting with gliders and motors. Now they thought they had the right combination, and so they had come to Kitty Hawk, a near-deserted island on the Outer Banks of North Carolina.

Four volunteers from the nearby U.S. Life Saving Station helped them lay the wooden track needed to launch the airplane, as they called it. With the plane ready and Orville lying in a sort of cradle on

the lower wing, they started the engine. The machine raced along the track, Wilbur steadying it as he ran alongside.

Suddenly the airplane rose into the air. It flew about 120 feet—almost twelve seconds—the first motor-driven, heavier-than-air machine under the control of man.

Wilbur flew the plane next. Altogether the brothers made four flights that day. Wilbur's final flight lasted fifty-nine seconds; he had flown 852 feet. On December 17, 1903, between the hours of 10:35 A.M. and 12:00 noon, the Wright brothers began the age of aviation.

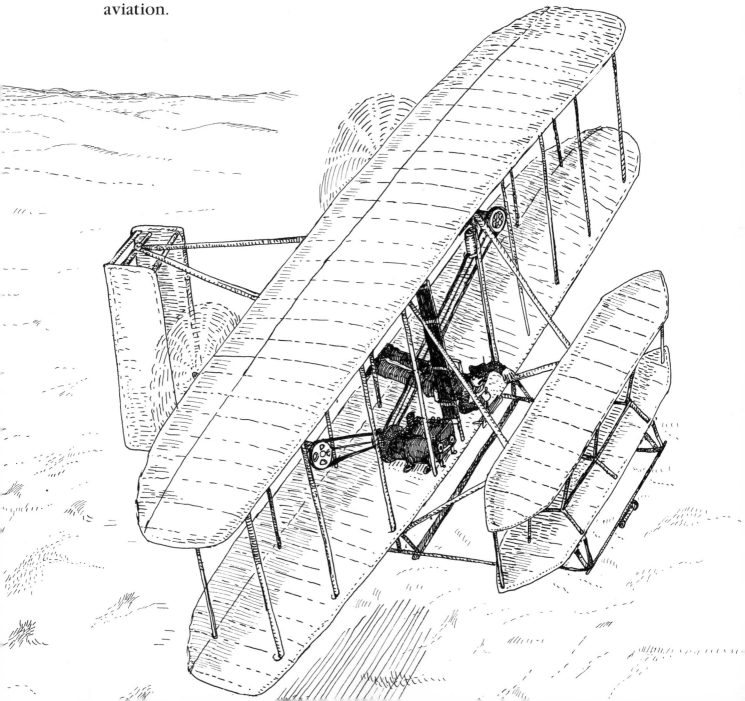

Europeans found it difficult to believe that an American had successfully flown an airplane. In October, 1906, Alberto Santos-Dumont, a wealthy young Brazilian living in France, built and flew a strange-looking biplane. His flights were much more limited than those of the Wright brothers, but Europeans hailed them as the world's first.

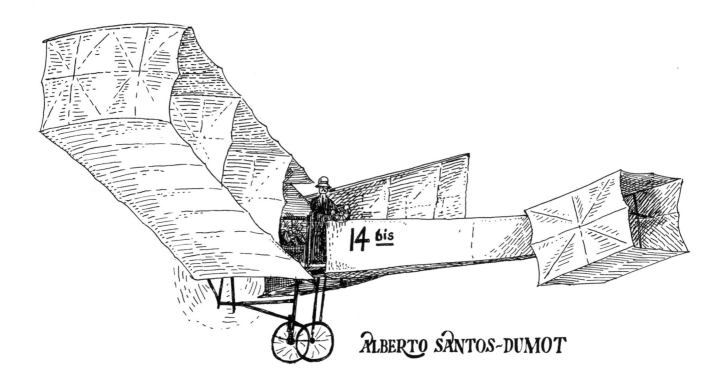

ALBERTO SANTOS-DUMOT

In America, the Wright brothers' chief competition was Glenn Curtiss. Together with Alexander Graham Bell, the inventor of the telephone, he built a successful airplane called the *June Bug*. Afterward, Curtis built the first practical seaplane. Moving to San Diego, he built seaplanes and trained pilots for the navy.

AN EARLY PILOT

GLENN CURTISS

Louis Blériot, a French automobile-lamp manufacturer, was determined to bring glory to France. An airplane enthusiast, he built his first plane in 1907. He kept flying and improving his designs, despite over fifty accidents.

On July 25, 1909, Blériot took off from Calais in his Model XI. He flew twenty-three miles and landed on a field near Dover Castle, becoming the first person to make winged flight across the English Channel. Blériot won a $5,000 prize. He also became a leading manufacturer of airplanes, as orders poured in for his monoplane.

A month after Blériot's flight, a great air meet was held at Reims, France. It was the first one ever. Almost everyone who was important in building and flying airplanes was there to compete, including Blériot, Glenn Curtiss, and a team representing the Wright brothers.

More than thirty planes took part in the meet, flying around the high wooden towers called pylons. They competed for trophies or prizes and new records were set for speed, altitude, and distance. Glenn Curtiss flew the fastest plane—47.65 m.p.h.—and Hubert Latham set the altitude mark of 508 feet.

The Reims air meet was a tremendous public success. It was also attended by the heads of many governments and their military advisors. Most came away convinced of the future importance of the airplane.

In January, 1911, Eugene Ely, a civilian test pilot working for Glenn Curtiss, landed his Curtiss biplane on a wooden platform built on the stern of the warship U.S.S. *Pennsylvania* in San Francisco Bay. Ely wore a football helmet for a crash helmet and tied bicycle-tire tubes around his chest as a life preserver. Ropes attached to sandbags stopped his forty-m.p.h. craft. It was the first aircraft-carrier landing.

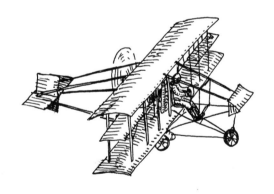

PENNSYLVANIA

WORLD WAR I

When the first World War started, airplanes were a little over ten years old. Most of the fighting nations had a variety of planes in their air forces, used mainly for observation and artillery spotting. When opposing pilots met in the air, they waved to each other and flew on—until the day one pilot shot at another with a pistol. Then the race began to build planes that could fly faster, farther, and higher than the enemy. The war was a great stimulus to aviation; technological developments that normally would have taken years were pushed through in months.

In the illustration, based on a contemporary painting by Henry Farre, the observer in a French Voisin defends his plane against a Fokker Eindecker by crawling out on the wing to avoid shooting his own rear-mounted pusher propeller.

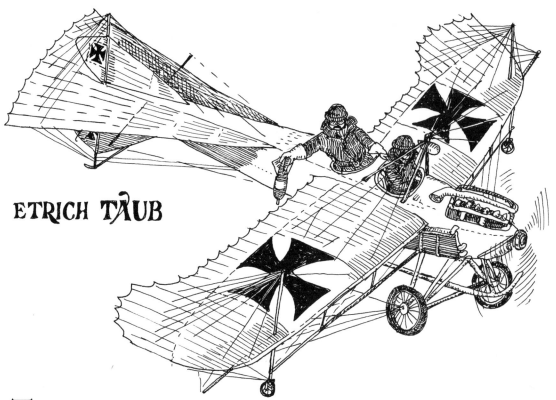

ETRICH TAUB

The first bombs ever dropped from an airplane were from Taubs, built by Germans, flown by Italians against the Turks, in Libya in 1911. In 1914, Parisians sitting in cafes at evening time and watching the regular bombing of Paris dubbed them "the Six-o-Clock Taubs."

The Fokker E-III—called the Eindecker or "one wing"—was the first great warplane designed by the Dutch airplane designer Anthony Fokker. Because of a secret invention which allowed machine-gun bullets to be fired between the blades of a spinning propeller, this plane ruled the air during the early part of the war.

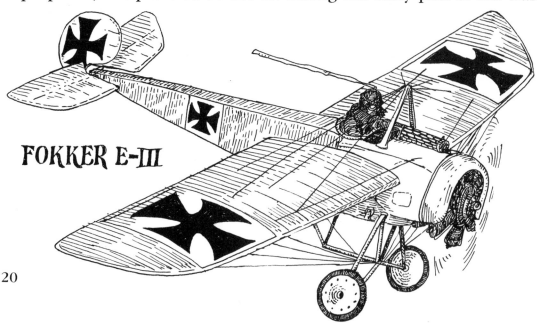

FOKKER E-III

FARMAN 1914

The Farman 1914 was used early in the war by the French, British, Italians, and Russians. It was lightly armed and used mainly as a bomber and for observation.

With its forward-firing Lewis machine gun, the fast-climbing DH-2 fighter reached the Western Front in late 1915, just in time to save the Allied air forces from complete destruction by the Fokker E-III.

DE HAVILLAND DH-2

1914~1915   1915~1917   1917~1918

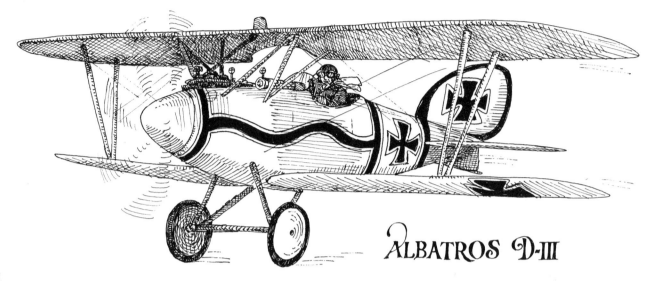

ALBATROS D-III

The Fokker DR-I, although a legendary plane, had a very limited life because it was difficult to fly. Only 320 were ever produced, but pilots like Manfred von Richthofen—the Red Baron—won many victories flying them.

Anthony Fokker's best effort, and probably the best fighter plane of World War I, was the Fokker D-VII, which appeared in 1917 and continued to fly in many air forces until the 1930s.

FOKKER DR-I

Flying the Albatros D-III, the German Air Force continued to dominate the skies. The basic unit of the air force was the jasta, which was equivalent to the British squadron, the French escadrille, or the Italian squadriglies. Each jasta identified itself by a color. Each pilot then decorated his plane to his own fancy, within the jasta's color scheme. These colorful groups helped earn the nickname "Flying Circuses."

FOKKER D-VII

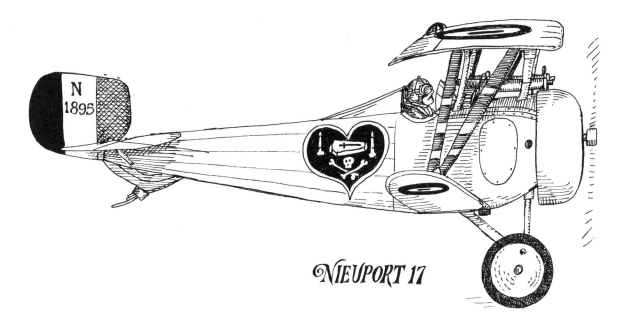

NIEUPORT 17

The Nieuports, first the Bebe and then the larger 17, were flown by many of the legendary Allied pilots, including French pilots Nungesser and Fonck, and British pilots Bishop and Ball. The Nieuports were able to meet the Eindecker and Albatros on equal terms.

The SPAD (the initials of its manufacturer, Societé pour Aviation et ses Derivés) was the best and most famous of the Allied pursuit planes. About 8,500 of them were built and they were equal to any plane the Germans put in the air. Eventually the SPADs were flown by all the French escadrilles, and the Americans flew them when they entered the war.

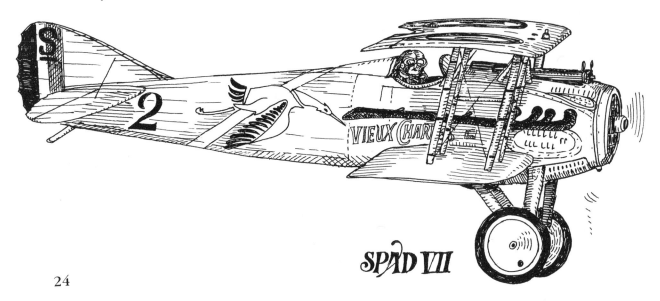

SPAD VII

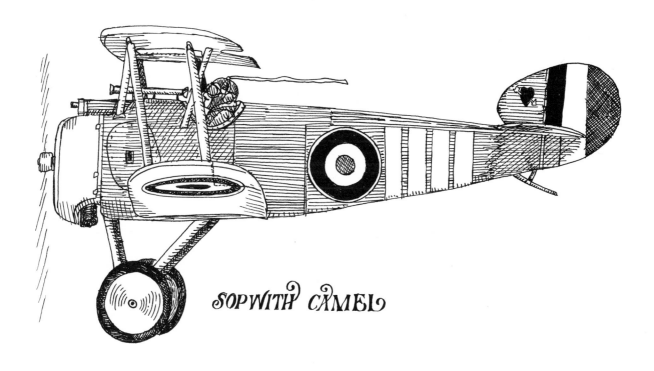

SOPWITH CAMEL

Fast and maneuverable, the Sopwith Camel was credited with the most victories of all the Allied planes—1,294 enemy planes downed. It was armed with two synchronized Vickers machine guns which were mounted in a hump in front of the pilot, hence the name "Camel."

The SE-5A was the other British fighter plane of distinction. Over 5,000 of these rugged fighters were built.

SE-5A

Italy was one of the pioneers in big bomber design. A two-wing Caproni Ca-3 was flying in 1914. The Ca-4 was designed later in the war. About forty of these three-wing monsters were built. Its three engines helped carry 3,900 pounds of bombs in a pod, or container, under the bottom wing.

This giant was used to bomb Austria, Italy's primary enemy during
World War I. Since the pilots and gunners sat in open cockpits, flying
over the Alps in winter was a job for only the strong and the brave.

27

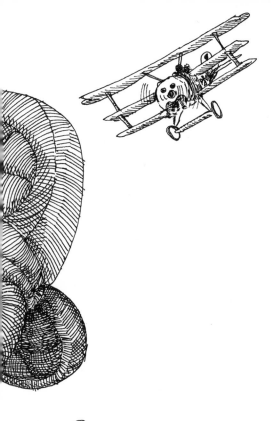

When the United States entered the war in April, 1917, it had very few trained pilots or flyable planes. When new aircraft production was planned and organized, the American squadrons were equipped with English and French planes.

Here Lieutenant Frank Luke in his SPAD 13 is about to attack a German observation balloon, a very dangerous undertaking. Observation balloons were connected to the ground by cables and quickly winched down when attacked. They were also heavily protected by flights of fighter planes. If the attacking pilot got through the enemy fighters, he had to face concentrated and very accurate antiaircraft cannons called "Archies." Frank Luke had eighteen victories to his credit, fourteen of them balloons, and he became known as the "Balloon Buster."

Count Ferdinand von Zeppelin was a famous designer and builder of giant airships—large balloons filled with inflammable hydrogen gas. Eventually, all dirigibles came to be called by his name: Zeppelins.

The German Naval Airship Service started bombing London in 1915. On moonless nights, squadrons of Zeppelins crossed the Channel to raid the city. But Sopwith Camels and DH-4s, equipped as night-fighters and firing incendiary bullets, quickly became effective against the intruders. The Zeppelins then tried for altitudes of up to 20,000 feet to avoid the fighters, but the crews suffered terribly from cold and lack of oxygen and the engines did not function well at those altitudes. Eventually, the Zeppelins were relegated to North Sea patrol and the raids against England were taken over by the Gotha G-IVs.

THE GOTHA G-IV

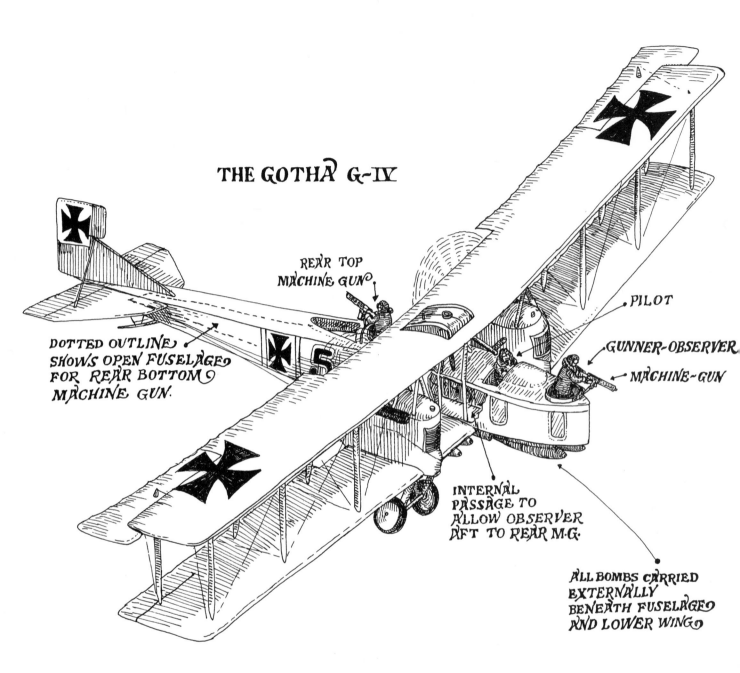

REAR TOP
MACHINE GUN

PILOT

GUNNER-OBSERVER

MACHINE-GUN

DOTTED OUTLINE
SHOWS OPEN FUSELAGE
FOR REAR BOTTOM
MACHINE GUN.

INTERNAL
PASSAGE TO
ALLOW OBSERVER
AFT TO REAR M.G.

ALL BOMBS CARRIED
EXTERNALLY
BENEATH FUSELAGE
AND LOWER WING

Powered by two Mercedes pusher engines, the Gotha bomber carried up to 1,000 pounds of bombs under the wings and fuselage. In June, 1917, squadrons of Gotha G-IVs started daylight bombing of London. The raids continued until the British brought the Sopwith Camel to the defense. The Germans then resorted to night bombing, which they continued on and off until the end of the war.

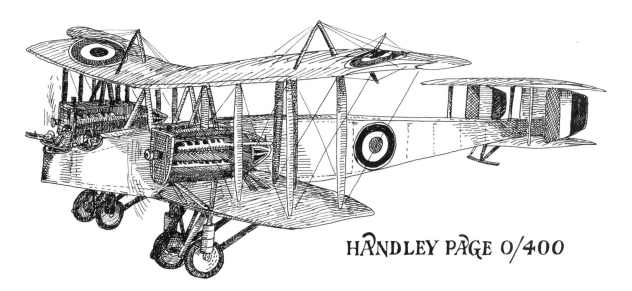

HANDLEY PAGE 0/400

The Handley Page was the first practical heavy night bomber to be used by either side. Spurred on by the Gotha bombings of London, hundreds of 0/400s were built. Capable of carrying a new 1,650-pound bomb called the "Blockbuster," squadrons of these bombers, flying from bases in France, delivered the war into Germany.

Named after a famous hero in Russian mythology, the Ilya Murometz was designed and first flown by Igor Sikorsky when he was twenty-three years old. Sikorsky emigrated to the United States after the war and became famous, first for his giant flying boats, and then for his helicopters.

ILYA MUROMETZ

DH-4

The de Havilland DH-4 was widely used as a bomber, photo-reconnaissance plane, and fighter. It was fast, well armed, and could fly at high altitudes, making it difficult for all but the best German fighters to challenge it.

CURTISS H-16 FLYING BOAT

The United States Navy and the British Royal Navy had an active role in the air war. Flying from bases in the Azores, France, and England, Curtiss H-12 and H-16 flying boats patrolled the Atlantic Ocean, the English Channel, and the North Sea. Armed with two depth charges and four machine guns, these flying boats were very successful in protecting convoys against German submarines.

FRANCE

103ᵈ ESCADRILLE
(SP·103)

48ᵗʰ ESCADRILLE (SP·48)

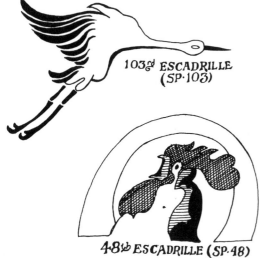

68ᵗʰ ESCADRILLE
(SP·68)

AVION DE
BOMBARDEMENT
B·M·119

ESCADRILLE DE CORPS DE ARMÉE
A·R·58

ESCADRILLE DE CHASSE SP·62

INSIGNIAS

Squadrons of both the Allies and the Central Powers had insignias proudly displayed on the fuselages of their planes. Classic examples are the various "Stork" escadrilles of the French Air Force, the "Indian Head" of the Lafayette Escadrille, and the legendary "Hat in Ring" of Captain Eddie Rickenbacker's 94th Pursuit Squadron. In the German jastas, the whole plane became the insignia.

111e ESCADRILLE OF
THE FRENCH AIR ARM

117e ESCADRILLE OF THE
MILITARY AIR ARM

GERMANY

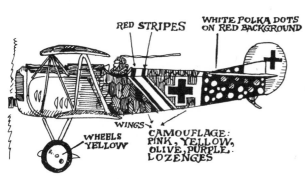

RED STRIPES

WHITE POLKA DOTS ON RED BACKGROUND

WINGS

WHEELS YELLOW

CAMOUFLAGE: PINK, YELLOW, OLIVE, PURPLE, LOZENGES

SOME GERMAN PILOTS' PERSONAL INSIGNIAS

THE UNITED STATES

22nd SQUADRON

94th SQUADRON

50th SQUADRON

96th BOMBER SQUADRON

213th SQUADRON

11th BOMBER SQUADRON

ITALY

1st RECONNAISSANCE SECTION

80th FIGHTER SQUADRIGLIA

4a SQUADRIGLIA

In order to survive, pilots had to have quick reflexes, as well as a great deal of luck, skill, and courage. The danger they faced daily was as much in the frailty of their aircraft as in combat. Although primitive parachutes had been developed, they were too big for pursuit planes. Fighter pilots had to be the victors to survive.

Pilots often dressed in dashing uniforms with white silk scarves wrapped around their necks. Many of their exploits recalled the days of chivalry. And their governments did much to glorify the heroes. Legends about pilots—some true and some propaganda—fired people's imaginations on the home front.

LIEUTENANT MAX IMMELMANN

Germany's first ace was Lieutenant Max Immelmann. Flying a Fokker Eindekker, he invented the "Immelmann turn," a maneuver which gave him the advantage during dogfights. When he was shot down, he had had fifteen victories.

MANFRED VON RICHTHOFEN

Baron Manfred von Richthofen was Germany's legendary ace of aces. Called the "Red Baron" because of the red Fokker DR-I he flew, von Richthofen amassed eighty victories, the most of any pilot during the war. Here he wears the *Pour le Merite,* also called the "Blue Max," Germany's highest decoration. On April 2, 1918, he was shot down by a Canadian, Captain Roy Brown. Richthofen landed behind British lines; his plane was intact but he was dead.

The indestructible Lieutenant Charles Nungesser was repeatedly wounded or injured in his four years as a combat pilot. He sustained a fractured skull, several fractures of the upper jaw, two of the lower jaw, broken ankles and wrists, a dislocated collarbone, and dislocation of both knees, as well as many bullet wounds in the arms, legs, and body. Nungesser ended the war as France's third leading ace. He disappeared in 1927 with a companion while trying to fly across the Atlantic Ocean.

This thin, frail French pilot was a national hero. France's second leading ace, he, too, was repeatedly wounded in combat, but always returned. In September, 1917, Captain Guynemer disappeared while flying a patrol. Neither his body nor his plane was ever found. All sorts of legends and stories were told of his disappearance and the French people refused to believe he was dead.

GEORGE GUYNEMER

René Fonck was France's leading ace with seventy-five victories. He was second only to von Richthofen as the leading ace of the war. Fonck survived the war and for a while he flew as a stunt pilot. Eventually he returned to the Air Service and retired as a general.

RENÉ FONCK

The Lafayette Escadrille was made up of Americans who volunteered to fly in the French Army. This squadron was activated in April, 1916, and remained in service until the United States entered the war. The Escadrille was then absorbed into the United States Air Service and became the 103rd Pursuit Squadron.

Raoul Lufbery was the ace of the Escadrille with seventeen victories. He was commissioned a major when he joined the Americans. Before he could gain a victory as a U.S. pilot, he was shot down by a German two-seater.

Raoul Lufbery driving an Hispano Suiza Roadster

The first British ace was Major Lanoe Hawker. He helped form the first British single-seat fighter unit and eventually claimed nine victories flying a DH-2 pusher. In a famous man-to-man duel with von Richthofen, he was shot down. He was the Baron's eleventh victim.

The list of British aces includes Englishmen, Canadians, Australians, Irishmen, Scots, Welshmen, and South Africans. There was a dispute about the leading ace. "Mick" Mannock claimed seventy-three victories before he was shot down in July, 1918. A Canadian, Billy Bishop, claimed seventy-two victories before he was ordered to return to Canada to help set up the new Canadian Air Force.

CAPTAIN BILLY BISHOP

Although the United States did not enter the war until April, 1917, many Americans were flying with the French and British. Captain Eddie Rickenbacker, with twenty-eight confirmed enemies shot down, was the leading U.S. ace. Rickenbacker was a famous racing-car driver before entering the service and he first went overseas as an officer's chauffeur. He transferred to the Air Service in France, where he received his flight training.

THE WAR IS OVER

When the war ended on November 11, 1918, most pilots found themselves out of a job. Trained by the thousands, they returned with a new skill and no place to work. There were few airplanes, no airlines, very few airports and just the beginnings of airmail service between some large cities. Few people had even seen an airplane and fewer still had flown in one.

The nation had just fought "the war to end all wars" and would not pay for an air force it thought it did not need. So, the Army Air Service sold thousands of surplus airplanes, mostly the Curtiss JN-4Ds. Many out-of-work pilots bought these cheap surplus "Jennies" and created a new American hero, the barnstormer. Flying all across the country, landing in cow pastures and barnyards, they kept themselves and their patched-up crates together by taking the local people up for rides. These legendary "gypsy pilots" brought aviation to every corner of America.

Traveling alone, or as part of a carnival, flying circuses went from town to town. These daredevils did stunt flying, wing walking, jumping from plane to plane and from speeding cars onto rope ladders suspended from Jennies. They raced. They flew upside down. They sent the thrill of flying through every watching crowd.

Here, wing walkers are dressed as clowns. The man hanging onto the landing gear will soon drop into the cockpit of the Jenny just taking off. Later, the two surplus World War I fighters, a SPAD and a Fokker, will perform mock dogfights for the crowd. After the show, people will be offered rides for as little as 50¢ a minute. They will be able to see their familiar towns and farms from the air.

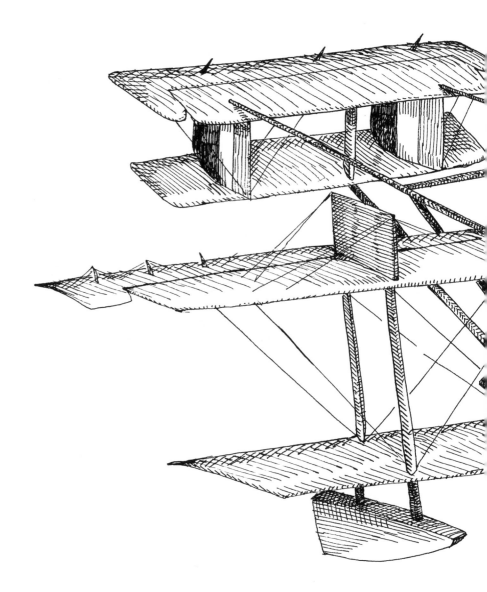

To sell the public on the idea of an air force, the army and navy began an era of exploration. Oceans were to be crossed, continents spanned, new altitude records established, and new speeds attained. Every new achievement brought headlines and helped to encourage Congress to spend money for new airplanes.

In 1919, the U.S. Navy commissioned three Curtiss seaplanes, *NC-1, NC-3,* and *NC-4,* to try to cross the Atlantic. The three planes

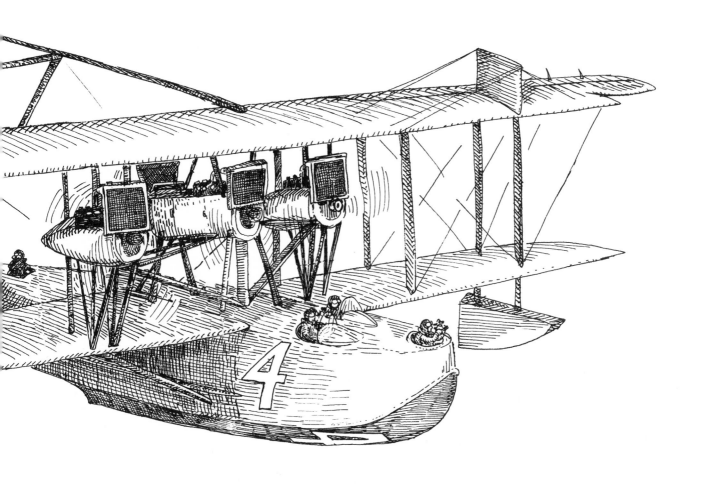

took off from Rockaway on Long Island and made their way to New-foundland. Then *NC-1* was forced down and sank off the Azores. *NC-3* also landed at sea, but taxied and drifted to the Azores. Only *NC-4* completed the trip from New York to Plymouth, England, via Newfoundland, the Azores, and Portugal. It took twenty-three days, although the actual flying time was fifty-four hours. *NC-4* was the first airplane to cross an ocean.

The Vickers Vimy was designed as a bomber but the war ended before the Vimy ever saw action. The plane would have served in the Royal Air Force's peacetime squadrons and then disappeared into history but for two historic flights.

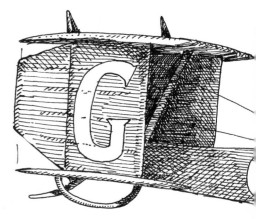

In June, 1919, two RAF pilots, Captain John Alcock and Lieutenant Arthur Whitten-Brown, flew a Vimy nonstop across the Atlantic from Newfoundland, crash-landing in a bog in Ireland. In November of the same year, two Australian officers serving in the RAF, Captain Ross Smith and his brother, Keith Smith, together with two mechanics, flew a Vimy from England to Australia. Great planning and special arrangements had to be made for the flight. Airstrips had to be built in remote places in the world and fuel and supplies sent ahead months in advance. The 11,000-mile flight took twenty-nine days. Their trip was filled with incredible adventures and near disasters.

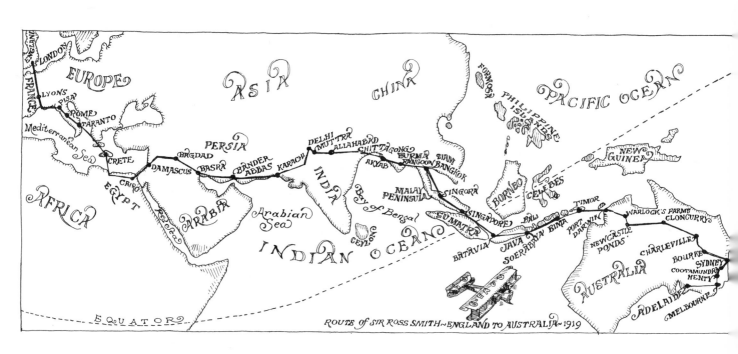

ROUTE OF SIR ROSS SMITH~ENGLAND TO AUSTRALIA~1919

Across the Southern Alps

In 1921, Army Lieutenant J. A. Macready set a new altitude record despite terrible hardships. Flying a specially built airplane, *Le Père,* he climbed to a new high of 34,508 feet. Macready's plane had an open, unheated cockpit. In spite of his army uniform, several suits of woolen underwear, a suit of leather padded with down and feathers, fur-lined gloves, fleece-lined boots over fur-lined moccasins, and goggles treated with antifreeze gelatin, Macready nearly froze to death.

In 1923, Lieutenant Macready and Lieutenant Oakley Kelly took off from Roosevelt Field in Long Island in a Fokker T-2 loaded with extra gasoline. Flying westward across rivers and prairies and between the Rocky Mountains—they couldn't gain enough altitude to fly over them—they were the first pilots to fly nonstop across the continent. The weary army pilots landed in California twenty-six hours and fifty minutes after takeoff. Their average speed was ninety-four m.p.h.

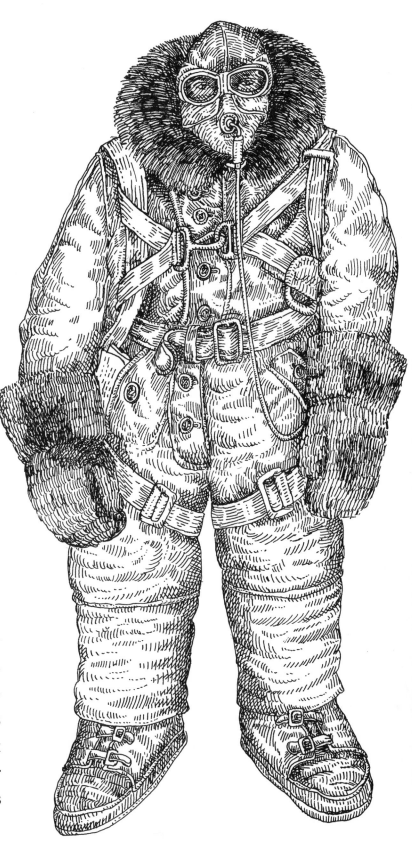

General Billy Mitchell had commanded the U.S. Air Service in Europe. He believed that bombers were the weapon of the future and he started a long feud with the navy about the importance of airplanes over battleships. The War Department set up an experiment to try to end the dispute. A captured German battleship, the impregnable *Ostfriesland,* was to be the target. Mitchell's bombers sank the ship in twenty-five minutes with a hail of 2,000-pound bombs. But the navy was still not convinced and the debate continued for years. It did not end even after General Mitchell's court-martial for insubordination in 1925.

Converted from a collier (coal carrier) in 1922, the U.S.S. *Langley* was the first aircraft carrier built by the U.S. Navy. A generation of navy pilots, "old Langley men," learned carrier flying and tactics on "Old Covered Wagon," as the *Langley* was nicknamed. Here, a Curtiss F2C takes off from the deck. It was the first fighter plane specially designed for landing and takeoff from a carrier. Converted to a seaplane tender during World War II, it was in service until sunk by the Japanese.

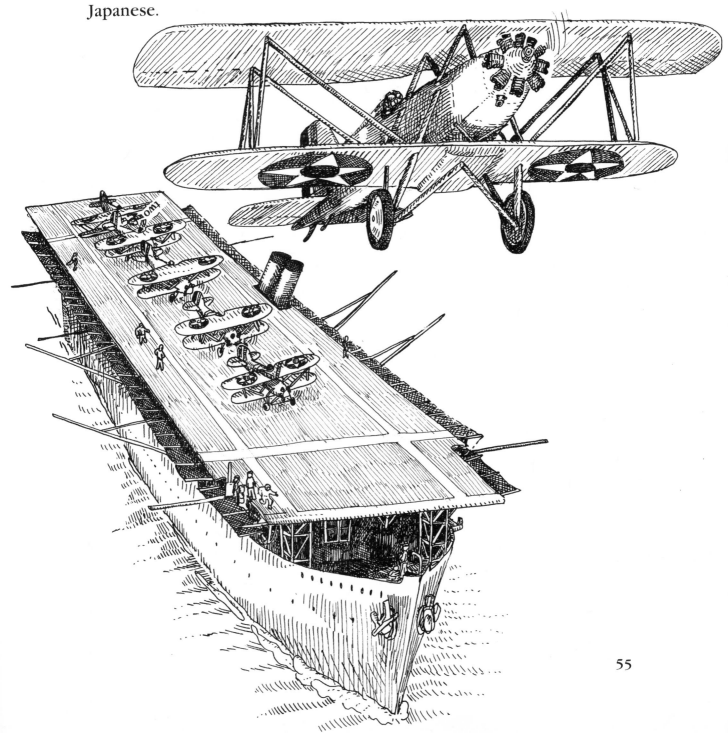

Under the guidance of General Billy Mitchell, the army prepared one of the most daring feats of the 1920s. Four planes specially built by the Douglas Aircraft Company would be the first to fly around the world.

The arrangements were started a year in advance. Twenty-two nations cooperated in the task and forty landing fields were prepared and stocked with supplies. Christened *Chicago, New Orleans, Boston,* and *Seattle,* the planes took off from a lake in Seattle, Washington, on April 26, 1924.

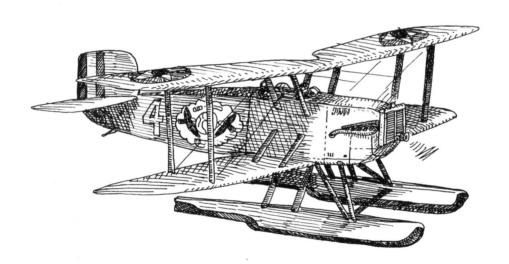

The first casualty was the *Seattle,* which smashed into an Alaskan mountainside. The crew survived and walked out of the wilderness in eleven days. The remaining three planes went on to Japan and across Asia. In Calcutta, their pontoons were exchanged for wheels. The "World Cruisers" then continued on from India to Persia, Asia Minor, the Balkans, then Paris and London. On the trip over the North Atlantic to Iceland, problems with a fuel pump caused *Boston* to be abandoned. But *New Orleans* and *Chicago* finished the flight and returned to Seattle five months after they left.

In 1925, the U.S. Postal Service inaugurated night flying as part of the coast-to-coast airmail service. Even though delivery time could be cut in half, cross-country night flying was unheard-of because it was so hazardous. In those days, pilots had few instruments for navigating in the dark.

First, a series of airports were built across the country about 300 miles apart, together with small emergency landing fields which were, in many cases, no more than pastures. The planes were mostly old DH-4s with the front cockpits removed for carrying the mail. Pilots wore parachutes and planes were equipped with flares for lighting emergency landings.

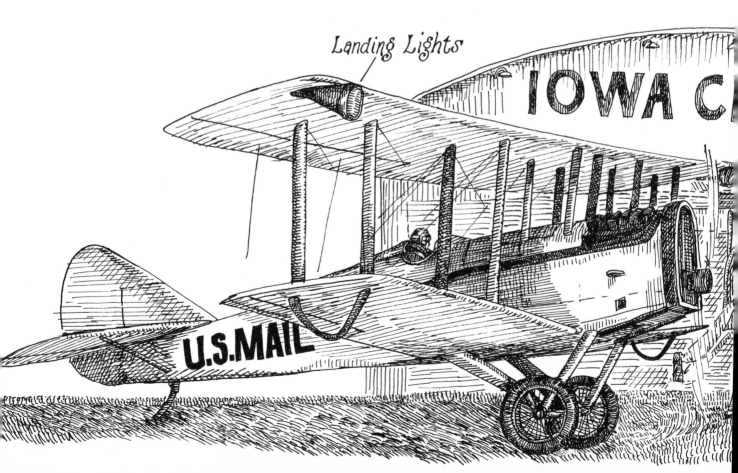

Landing Lights

IOWA C

U.S.MAIL

Thus began another group of brave and romantic fliers, the legendary airmail pilots. Flying over mountains and deserts in all sorts of weather, from blizzards to sandstorms, these pilots maintained their schedules and delivered the mail. They were paid $1,764 a year, plus 5¢ to 7¢ a mile, depending on the difficulty of the route. Night flying paid double.

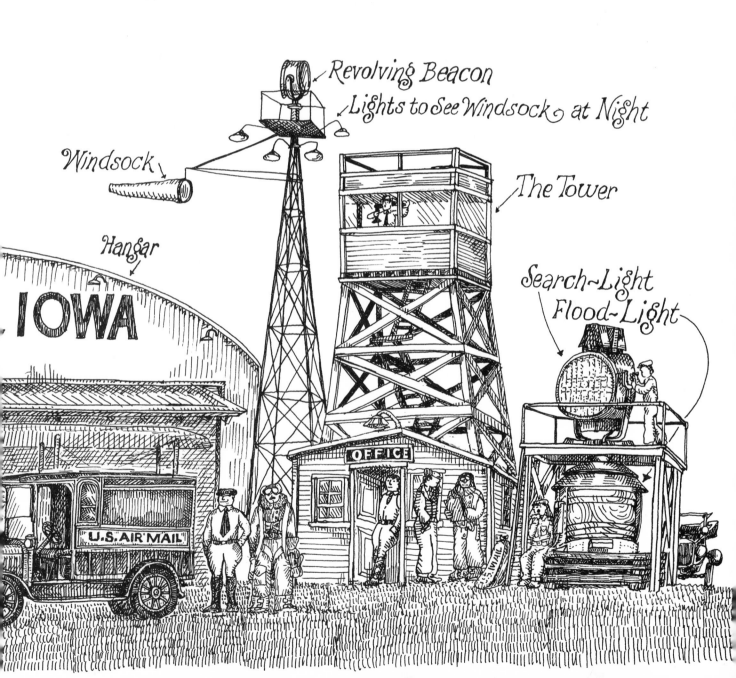

The race was on to be the first to fly over the North Pole. On frigid Spitzbergen, an island off Norway, Commander Richard Byrd and his pilot, Floyd Bennett, were assembling their tri-motored Fokker, equipped with ski-landing gear. Also preparing for the trip was the famous explorer Roald Amundsen. He would attempt the trip in a dirigible commanded by an Italian general, Umberto Nobile.

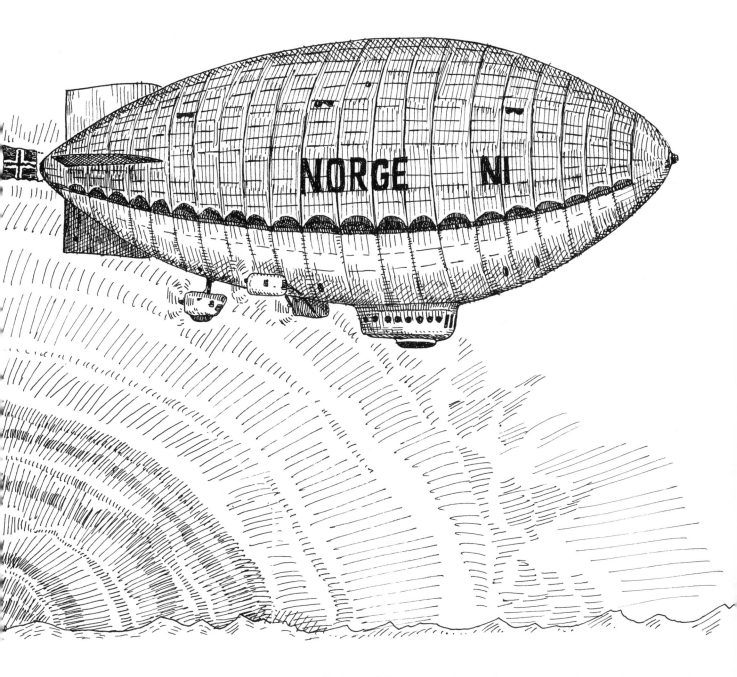

Byrd and Bennett took off first. They navigated over uncharted Arctic wastes to the North Pole and then flew back. The next day, Amundsen and his crew left Spitzbergen. They, too, flew over the Pole but then continued on over the top of the world to Point Barrow, Alaska. Although Byrd and Bennett were the first to fly over the North Pole, Amundsen's feat is acknowledged an equal victory.

Charles Lindbergh was an ex-barnstormer. He was also an airmail pilot with over 2,000 hours of perilous flying experience. He was twenty-four years old.

On May 20, 1927, a group of aviators had gathered at Roosevelt Field, Long Island. They were hoping to be the first to fly nonstop across the Atlantic from New York to Paris. Lindbergh got the first jump. He took off from a rain-soaked field into a misty morning, his Ryan monoplane, *The Spirit of St. Louis,* just clearing the telephone wires and treetops.

Lindbergh reached Newfoundland around dusk and headed out over the North Atlantic. Fighting fatigue and exhaustion, trying to stay awake, he flew on through the endless night. At dawn he spotted

fishing boats and then the coast of Ireland. He'd done it! Continuing on across England to Paris, he landed at Le Bourget airport 33 1/2 hours after takeoff.

At Le Bourget, the police were unable to restrain the thousands of people as they tore souvenirs from the plane and bore Lindbergh off on their shoulders. Wild and enthusiastic welcomes in other European cities followed, but the most spectacular welcome was given by millions of New Yorkers in a tremendous tickertape parade down Broadway on his triumphant return to America.

Lindbergh's flight captured the imagination of the world. People everywhere called him the "Lone Eagle" and he became a national hero. His daring flight came to symbolize a new pioneer spirit in aviation and in America. A whole new era was about to begin and pilots like Lindbergh would lead the way.

INDEX

64